Kate Pankhurst

BLOOMSBURY
CHILDREN'S BOOKS
LONDON OXFORD NEW YORK NEW DELHI SYDNEY

OFFICIAL MEMO

THE FANTASTICALLY GREAT SOCIETY

FGS HQ
SKY HIGH
HEIGHTS
CH8 NG3

Dear fantastically great reader,

You are receiving this letter because we at the **FANTASTICALLY GREAT SOCIETY** think you have what it takes to make a difference! Therefore, we would like to welcome you as our **NEWEST** member.

Our society was founded to celebrate and share the stories of people whose courage, creativity and brilliance shine in ways the world deserves to hear and remember. Why? Because when these stories are passed on, the next generation (that's you) can rise through our ranks with the super-skills and powerful knowledge needed to ...

CHANGE THE WORLD FOR THE BETTER
(or, in other words: be fantastically great!)

We are with you for every step of this thrilling journey – because when we stand together, truly remarkable things can happen.

OFFICE OF THE FANTASTICALLY GREAT SOCIETY

You will shortly receive words of wisdom and encouragement from a selection of the society's most experienced members. They have been called upon because they are highly skilled in a variety of essential world-changing areas, including:

- CREATIVITY and SELF-EXPRESSION
- SCIENTIFIC DISCOVERY
- STANDING UP FOR CHANGE
- WILD ADVENTURING
- EXTRAORDINARY IMAGINATION
- MAKING YOUR VOICE HEARD!

So, are you ready to learn, be inspired and harness everything that makes you **FANTASTICALLY GREAT**? Welcome to the club!

Yours inspiringly,

THE FANTASTICALLY GREAT SOCIETY

P.S. So you can learn more about each woman, we have enclosed the top secret case files we hold about their lives.

P.P.S. Our society is open to all, no matter your age, gender or dream!

OFFICE OF THE FANTASTICALLY GREAT SOCIETY

MEMBER No. 200

Frida Kahlo

OFFICIAL PORTRAIT
MEMBER NUMBER: 200

When Frida was six, she caught polio – an illness that made one of her legs weaker than the other and caused her pain throughout her life. Despite this, she worked hard at school and dreamed of becoming a doctor. But at eighteen, she was badly hurt in a traffic accident. She recovered, but was left in constant pain and unable to have children.

Frida learned to paint during her recovery using a special easel and mirrors attached to her sick bed. Painting helped her feel better and for the rest of her life, she would use her art to help her cope with her suffering.

MEMBERSHIP DETAILS

NAME: Frida Kahlo
(**birth name:** Magdalena Carmen Frieda Kahlo y Calderón)

DATE OF BIRTH: 6 July ~~1910~~ 1907

NOTE: Frida sometimes said she was born in 1910 so her birth year would match the start of the Mexican Revolution. This isn't true – she was actually born three years earlier!

NATIONALITY: Mexican

OCCUPATION: Artist

FAMILY: I married Diego Rivera (twice!). He was sometimes my frenemy, but also my greatest love!

DESCRIBE YOURSELF IN 3 WORDS: Creative, fiery, unconventional!

GREATEST ACHIEVEMENT: Making the world sit up and notice Mexican artists

WORLD FIRSTS:
1. The first twentieth-century Mexican artist to have work included in the Louvre
2. The first Latin American artist whose work sold for more than $1 million at auction (for 'Diego y yo')

FAVOURITE ANIMAL: Dogs and monkeys (I had other pets too, but I loved these ones the most)

FAMOUS WORDS: "I am my own muse, the subject I know best."

YOU'RE INVITED!
EXHIBITION BY 31 WOMEN

Venue: 'Art of This Century' Gallery, West 57th Street, New York City. Jan 5–31 1943

Details: A radical, all-woman exhibition of abstract and surrealist artworks

Artists: Only women! Including Mexican artist, Frida Kahlo

RSVP: Peggy Guggenheim (art collector)

Increasingly, Frida began painting in the style of Mexican folk art, using bright colours and simply drawn subjects. One of her favourite things to paint was herself! Frida did lots of self-portraits, and liked to exaggerate her features, especially her eyebrows and facial hair. She loved her pets, and included them in many paintings to show how important family was to her and as symbols of her thoughts and feelings.

SELF-PORTRAIT WITH MONKEYS, 1943

Over her life, Frida created more than 200 artworks, many of which are now famous all over the world. She laughed a lot, but was often in poor health. Her last painting included the words *"Viva la Vida"*, meaning 'Long Live Life!' There was much sadness in Frida's life, but she turned her experiences into unique and wonderful works of art. This is what made her one of the most important artists of all time.

ITZCUINTLI DOG WITH ME, 1938

VIVA LA VIDA, WATERMELONS, 1954

TIMELINE

6 July 1907 – Born near Mexico City, Mexico

1910 – Mexican Revolution breaks out

1913 – Falls ill with polio

1925 – Injured in a bus accident and takes up painting

1927 – Joins Mexican Communist Party

1929 – Marries Diego Rivera

1938 – First solo exhibition at New York's Julien Levy Gallery

1939 – Divorces Diego. The Louvre art gallery in Paris buys Frida's self-portrait 'The Frame'

1939 – Remarries Diego

1946 – Awarded the National Prize of Arts and Sciences

13 July 1954 – Dies at the age of 47

THE FANTASTICALLY GREAT SOCIETY

OFFICIAL MEMO

FGS HQ
SKY HIGH
HEIGHTS
CH8 NG3

Dear Frida,

It is vitally important that our future members feel confident enough to **be their truly fantastic selves.** As you know, this is key to fulfilling one's incredible potential.

We at the society are in awe of how you have used art to explore your innermost thoughts and feelings – all the things that make you unique. You saw life in your own wonderful way and this helped you be resilient in the face of great challenges. Any tips you can share for how to encourage future members to do the same would be greatly appreciated.

Yours uniquely,

THE FANTASTICALLY GREAT SOCIETY

P.S. See you at the opening of your next art show! For now, viva la vida y adios!

CORREO AEREO
The AMAZING ARTIST!
YOUR SKETCHBOOK
CREATIV-CITY
ART Y1

MEMBER No. 88

Marie Curie

OFFICIAL PORTRAIT
MEMBER NUMBER: 88

MEMBERSHIP DETAILS

NAME: Maria Skłodowska-Curie (but you probably know me as Marie Curie!)

NOTE: Her parents named her 'Maria', but when she moved to Paris she started calling herself 'Marie' to feel more at home among the French.

DATE OF BIRTH: 7 November 1867

NATIONALITY: Polish, but I moved to France for university and eventually became a citizen

OCCUPATION: Scientist (a chemist and physicist)

FAMILY: I married Pierre Curie (my partner in life and in science!) in 1895. We had two children together – Ève Curie and Irène Joliot-Curie

DESCRIBE YOURSELF IN 3 WORDS: Inquisitive, passionate, determined

GREATEST ACHIEVEMENT: Discovering the wonder element radium, which meant doctors could finally start to treat cancer!

WORLD FIRSTS:

1. First woman to win a Nobel Prize (and the first person to be awarded the prize twice)
2. Only person to win a Nobel Prize in two scientific fields
3. First woman in France to get a PhD and first female professor at the Sorbonne University

FAVOURITE COLOUR: Green! I loved the green glow of "my beautiful radium", my favourite of the elements.

FAMOUS WORDS: "Nothing in life is to be feared, it is only to be understood."

Marie came from a poor family in Poland. She was a brilliant student and always desperate to learn. At the time, Polish universities didn't accept women, so Marie saved up to study science at university in Paris, France. It was a struggle, but she did it!

She began researching a recent scientific discovery ... **X-rays**! This led Marie to study another type of invisible ray (Becquerel rays) given off by the element uranium. Becquerel rays were thought to be produced by chemical reactions, but Marie wondered if they came from uranium atoms themselves. Soon, she realised lots of elements emitted invisible rays, and she called these elements 'radioactive'.

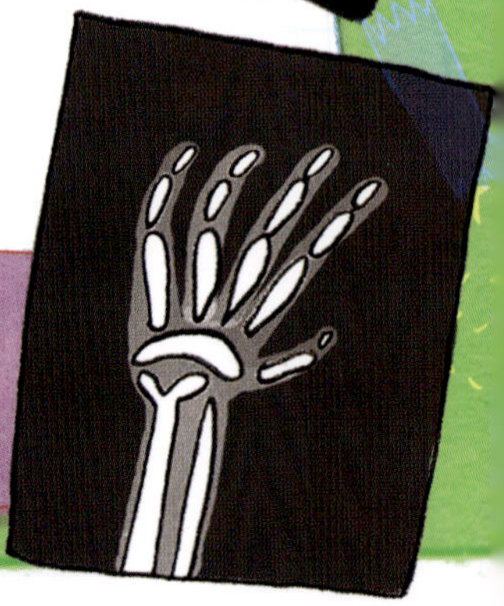

X-rays are invisible rays of energy that pass through the air and even through solid objects, like our bodies. They are a type of 'radiation'.

Marie's work made headlines when she discovered two new radioactive elements – polonium and radium. Excitingly, radium could be used to treat people with cancer. Unfortunately, radium was also dangerous (though Marie and Pierre didn't know it yet). Marie felt ill a lot of the time because she was suffering from radiation poisoning.

For her brilliant work, Marie was awarded a Nobel Prize – twice! Today, she is remembered as one of the most influential scientists who ever lived.

Ra

Po

THE NEWS TODAY, October 1914, France

MARIE CURIE: WARTIME HERO!

Scientist Marie Curie made a brilliant contribution to the WW1 war effort by launching her special mobile X-ray machines.

Known as 'Petites Curies', these machines were driven by Marie to the front line to X-ray wounded soldiers.

TIMELINE

7 November 1867 – Born in Warsaw, Poland (then known as 'Congress Poland', part of the Russian Empire)

1891 – Leaves Warsaw to study at the Sorbonne, a renowned French university

1894 – Denied a job at Kraków University because she is a woman

1895 – Marries Pierre Curie

1898 – Marie and Pierre discover polonium (named after Marie's home country, Poland) and radium

1903 – Receives the Nobel Prize in Physics

1906 – Pierre dies in a traffic accident. Marie takes over his position as Professor of General Physics at the Sorbonne

1911 – Receives the Nobel Prize in Chemistry

1914–1918 – Develops portable X-ray units used in World War One

4 July 1934 – Dies at age 66 from an illness likely caused by exposure to radiation

And the winner of the 1911 Nobel Prize in chemistry is ...

Marie Curie!

In 1903, Marie became the first woman to win a Nobel Prize (that time, in Physics). Then, she won another one in 1911, making her the only person to be awarded a Nobel Prize in two different sciences.

Marie with her Nobel Prize medals

RADIUM

OFFICIAL MEMO

THE FANTASTICALLY GREAT SOCIETY

FGS HQ
SKY HIGH
HEIGHTS
CH8 NG3

Dear Marie,

We want our newest recruits to fizz with the same unstoppable curiosity that powered your work! It's the spark that kept you asking questions when experiments were long and difficult – and when people tried to tell you that someone like you shouldn't be doing science at all.

Your world-changing discoveries show exactly why science must be open to everyone (how completely OUTRAGEOUS that anyone ever claimed women weren't capable of being brilliant scientists)! So, dear Marie, we would be in our element if you would share some wisdom from your lab to inspire even more fantastically great thinkers!

Radiating gratitude,

THE FANTASTICALLY GREAT SOCIETY

DANGER! RADIATION!

OFFICIAL SOCIETY EXPERIMENT

THE FANTASTICALLY GREAT SOCIETY

Marie Curie
Institut du Radium
1 Rue Pierre et Marie Curie
Paris
FRANCE

PARIS - 02-MAY 1927 - FRANCE

Po

Ra

X-RAY
1st
Brilliant Young Scientist
Laboratory No.9
T3ST TU8E

Rosa Parks

MEMBERSHIP DETAILS

NAME: Rosa Parks

DATE OF BIRTH: 4 February 1913

NATIONALITY: American

OCCUPATION: Seamstress and civil rights activist

FAMILY: My mother, grandparents and little brother, who protected me and taught me so much. At 19, I also married Raymond Parks, a fellow activist!

DESCRIBE YOURSELF IN 3 WORDS: Courageous, principled, bold

GREATEST ACHIEVEMENT: Sparking a movement that helped change laws that discriminated against black people

WORLD FIRSTS: Segregation laws in Alabama first changed because of a movement that I started!

FAVOURITE FOOD: Peanut butter – especially with my famous 'featherlite pancakes'

FAMOUS WORDS: "The only tired I was, was tired of giving in."

OFFICIAL PORTRAIT
MEMBER NUMBER: 381

Growing up on her grandparents' farm in Alabama, Rosa Parks understood discrimination from a young age. Strict laws called 'Jim Crow Laws' meant black and white people had to use separate facilities – these even included schools and drinking fountains! This was known as **segregation**. This discrimination made Rosa very angry, and when she was older, she joined a special organisation that hoped to end segregation of black and white people forever.

Rosa took a bus to work every day, but was only allowed on the seats for black people. One day, her bus was full and there were no seats left for white passengers, so the driver told Rosa to give up her seat. But she refused! She didn't argue or make a fuss, but she wouldn't budge. Eventually, the driver called the police and Rosa was arrested.

STOP PRESS : Bus Boycott Ends

After 381 days, the Montgomery Bus Boycott has officially ended, as has the bus segregation law. From today, 21 December 1956, all black and white passengers will have equal rights when riding city buses.

Lots of people were angry about Rosa's arrest. They thought the laws were unfair too! To support Rosa, they all boycotted (refused to use) the city buses until segregation on buses ended.

Eventually that law, and many other unfair laws, were changed. By kick-starting this campaign of peaceful, political protest, Rosa took an important step towards making the lives of black and white people equal.

TIMELINE

4 February 1913 – Born in Tuskegee in Alabama, USA

1932 – Marries Raymond Parks

1943–1957 – Serves as secretary and youth leader to Montgomery's National Association for the Advancement of Coloured People (NAACP)

December 1955 – Arrested and charged with violating segregation laws by not giving up her bus seat. Montgomery Bus Boycott begins

January 1956 – Loses department store job due to involvement in Montgomery Bus Boycott

November 1956 – US Supreme Court rules that segregation on buses must be stopped

1963 – Participated in the march on Washington for Jobs and Freedom

1964 – Segregation in America banned with passing of Civil Rights Act of 1964

1979–1999 – Awarded the NAACP Spingarn Medal, the Presidential Medal of Freedom and the Congressional Gold Medal

1987 – Founded the Rosa and Raymond Parks Institute for Self Development

24 October 2005 – Dies at age 92

NOTE: Rosa's original recipe uses two tablespoons, but you really only need two teaspoons!

Rosa Parks' 'Featherlite Pancakes' recipe

1. First sift together:
   - 1 cup flour
   - 2 teaspoons baking powder
   - 1/2 teaspoon salt
   - 2 tablespoons sugar
2. Then mix together:
   - 1 egg
   - 1 1/4 cup milk
   - 1/3 cup peanut butter, melted
3. Combine wet mix with dry ingredients
4. Grease a pan with one tablespoon cooking oil and cook mixture on medium heat (I like 275 °F on my griddle!)

NOTE: If you want to try this recipe, make sure to ask a grown-up to help you.

OFFICIAL MEMO

THE FANTASTICALLY GREAT SOCIETY

FGS HQ
SKY HIGH
HEIGHTS
CH8 NG3

Dear Rosa,

A **TOP PRIORITY** for our society is making sure our new members know just how important their actions can be. They might not always feel it, but we can all play a part in making the world a fairer place. Just as your dignified protest showed, one small, calm action can create an extraordinary ripple effect (with no shouting required)!

We would therefore be honoured if you could share some wisdom with the next generation of changemakers, helping them to find the courage and composure to make a mark of their own. To stand up (or sit down!) for what they care about, and realise just how powerful even the quietest action can be.

With you in quiet, but fierce determination,

THE FANTASTICALLY GREAT SOCIETY

P.S. We can't wait to read your advice!

Throughout her climbing career, Junko was supported by her devoted husband, Masanobu, who looked after their children while she went on expeditions. This was very unusual in Japan. Junko changed ideas of what was possible for Japanese women, and has inspired countless others to follow their dreams and not worry about what anyone thinks.

Congratulations to

JUNKO TABEI

For being the first woman to reach the summit of Mount Everest!

Date: 16 May 1975
Time: 12.30 p.m.
Sherpa guide: Ang Tsering
Ranking: 36th person to reach the summit

MEMBERSHIP CARD
JOSHI-TOHAN CLUB

NAME: Junko Tabei

MOTTO: Let's go on an overseas expedition by ourselves!

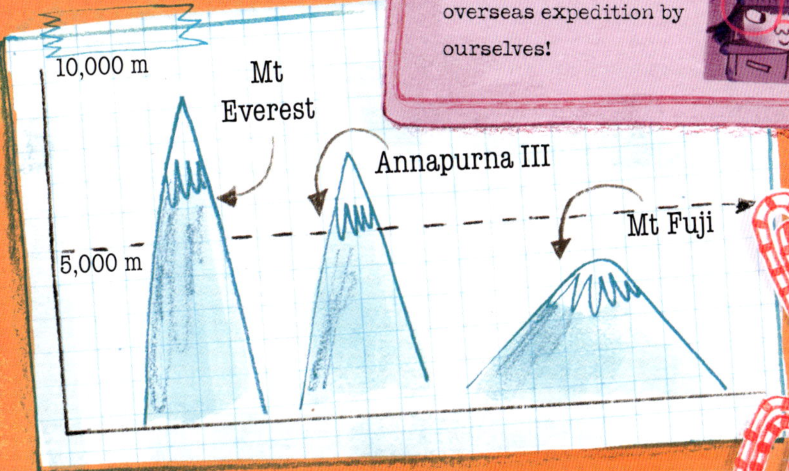

TIMELINE

22 September 1939 – Born in Miharu, near Fukushima, Japan

1939–1945 – World War Two

1949 – Attends a school climbing trip to Mount Nasu

1962 – Graduates from Showa Women's University

1965 – Marries Masanobu Tabei, a fellow mountaineer

1969 – Starts Japan's first women-only mountaineering club, Joshi-Tohan Club

1970 – Joshi-Tohan Club successfully climbs Annapurna III

16 May 1975 – Becomes the first woman to reach the top of Mount Everest

1990 – Sets up the Himalayan Adventure Trust of Japan, an NGO to protect the environment on Everest

1992 – Becomes first woman to complete the Seven Summits Challenge

1995 – Founded and chaired the first Women on Everest Summit Conference

2000 – Studies environmental science at Kyushu University in Japan

20 October 2016 – Dies at age 77

YAK MAIL

MT. EVEREST · BASE CAMP · 1975 · NEPAL

Junko Tabei
Everest Base Camp
Khumbu Glacier
NEPAL

URGENT POST

Junko's first hike, a school trip in 1949

OFFICIAL MEMO

THE FANTASTICALLY GREAT SOCIETY

FGS HQ
SKY HIGH
HEIGHTS
CH8 NG3

Hello up there, Junko!

We are writing with exciting news of your next great expedition! There are a growing number of ambitious young society members keen to embrace all the adventure that life has to offer. They will of course require an expert guide. Are you up for the challenge?

You were oh-so DARING! Refusing to listen to those who said the dangers were too much, especially for a woman. You were wildly DETERMINED – battling through blizzards, avalanches and bitter cold. You helped your team, and they helped you to reach your goal. That's why, no matter their adventure in life, our recruits will be ready for the journey with you!

See you on top of the world,

THE FANTASTICALLY GREAT SOCIETY

P.S. Give the yak we sent to deliver this letter a pat on the head from us!

Junko, sheltering at base camp

THINK BIG
FIRST CLASS
1st
A fellow DREAMER
Desk-in-the-Corner
Big Ideas
Wild Imagination

MEMBER No. 8849

JUNKO TABEI

OFFICIAL PORTRAIT
MEMBER NUMBER: 8849

MEMBERSHIP DETAILS

NAME: Junko Tabei

DATE OF BIRTH: 22 September 1939

NATIONALITY: Japanese

OCCUPATION: Mountaineer and environmentalist

FAMILY: My husband, Masanobu (my biggest supporter), and our two children, Noriko and Shinya

DESCRIBE YOURSELF IN 3 WORDS: Fearless, determined, strong

GREATEST ACHIEVEMENT: Showing other Japanese women that they can break the mould and follow their own dreams

WORLD FIRSTS:

1. First woman to reach the top of Mount Everest
2. First woman to complete the Seven Summits (the highest peak on each of the seven continents)
3. Part of the first women's group to climb Annapurna III

FAVOURITE MOUNTAIN: As much as I love Everest, it has to be Mount Fuji. One of the first big mountains I ever climbed and in my home country, too

FAMOUS WORDS: "Technique and ability alone do not get you to the top; it is the willpower that is most important."

As a small and not very strong child, Junko Tabei never imagined she could enjoy any sport ... until, aged ten, she went on a school climbing trip to Mount Nasu near her home in Miharu, Japan. There, Junko discovered she loved climbing! She could spend time in nature, and challenge herself rather than compete against others.

After university, Junko joined lots of climbing clubs. It was a very male-dominated hobby and many men disapproved of a woman trying to climb. But Junko didn't care. Soon, she had climbed all the biggest mountains in Japan! She also set up a climbing group just for women, which became the first female group to successfully climb the mountain Annapurna III. Five years later, Junko became the first woman to reach the top of Mount Everest!

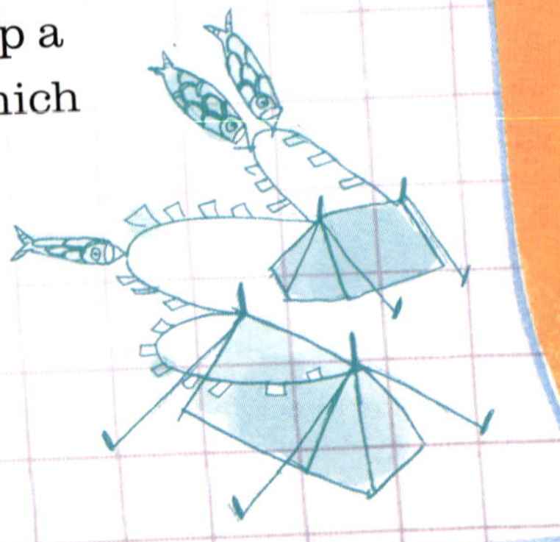

ONE WAY
NEXT STOP
CHANGE
USA POST
Alabama
6¢
A Changemaker
Back of the Bus
Winding Road
Bus Stop No. 37

ADA LOVELACE

MEMBERSHIP DETAILS

NAME: Augusta Ada King, Countess of Lovelace – or 'Enchantress of Numbers' as Charles used to call me

DATE OF BIRTH: 10 December 1815

NATIONALITY: British

OCCUPATION: Mathematician and writer

FAMILY: Married William King and had three children – Byron, Ralph Gordon and Anne Isabella – named after my parents, Anne Byron and George Gordon Byron (better known as the poet Lord Byron!)

DESCRIBE YOURSELF IN 3 WORDS:
Imaginative, analytical, visionary

GREATEST ACHIEVEMENT: The lasting legacy of my ideas, which have inspired people all over the world – especially girls – to see that they can be amazing at maths, science and invention too!

WORLD FIRSTS:
Wrote the world's first published computer algorithm, which kind of makes me the first ever computer programmer!

FAVOURITE ANIMAL: My cat, Mrs Puff! And birds – I love watching them fly, and even tried to copy them by making my own flying machine!

FAMOUS WORDS: "Your best and wisest refuge from all troubles is in your science."

Ada Lovelace grew up during an age of invention, when amazing machines were created to do things faster and better than any human. Luckily, Ada was a brilliant mathematician with an astounding imagination, so her mind was perfectly suited to delving into the possibilities that these machines had to offer. She even invented her own steam-powered flying machine when she was just twelve!

She became friends with a mathematician called Charles Babbage, who had just invented a huge mechanical calculator called the Difference Engine. Soon after, he revealed plans for an even better calculating creation – the Analytical Engine. But Ada realised it could do more than just make calculations. It could be instructed, or programmed, to carry out many other tasks as well.

OFFICIAL PORTRAIT
MEMBER NUMBER: 1843

BOOK REVIEW

Ada Lovelace's translation of an article about the Analytical Engine, published in 1843, includes many original ideas of her own about how this machine could work. Her brilliant insights (almost three times as long as the original article!) make this publication Ada's greatest contribution to computer science.

Without knowing it, Ada had predicted the age of computers. She even created a pattern of instructions – or 'algorithm' – that could be read by the Analytical Engine. This is now considered the first computer program! Sadly, the machine was too expensive to build, so Ada's vision never became a reality. But her contribution to computer science was a hundred years ahead of its time.

In a letter to her mother on **7 April 1828**, when she was just twelve, Ada wrote:

"I have got a scheme to make a thing in the form of a horse with a steam engine in the inside so contrived as to move an immense pair of wings, fixed on the outside of the horse, in such a manner as to carry it up into the air while a person sits on its back."

TIMELINE

10 December 1815 – Born in London, England

1816 – Her parents, Lady Annabella and Lord Byron, separate

1828 – Writes *Flyology*, a book of studies which includes designs for a flying machine

1829 – Suffers a severe bout of measles

5 June 1833 – Meets Charles Babbage and sees the Difference Engine

8 July 1835 – Marries William King (who later becomes 1st Earl of Lovelace)

1841-1843 – Publishes her translation of an article about the Analytical Engine. Her extensive 'Notes' include the first algorithm for a machine

1848 – Revolutions spread across Europe, with people demanding more rights and freedoms

1851 – The first World's Fair (Great Exhibition) is held in London, celebrating industrial progress

27 November 1852 – Becomes ill and dies at age 36

OFFICIAL MEMO

THE FANTASTICALLY GREAT SOCIETY

FGS HQ
SKY HIGH
HEIGHTS
CH8 NG3

Dearest Ada,

Your steam-powered ideas about computer programs were years ahead of their time! For the benefit of our newest recruits, who could learn so much about the wondrous possibility of imagination from you, we do hope this post manages to keep up with you!

Your sparky teamwork with inventor Charles Babbage made history! Are you ready for your next great collaboration? This time, with the brilliant brains of the society's newest members? Just think where their bright minds could take us, now and in years to come ...

Looking to an impossibly brilliant future,

THE FANTASTICALLY GREAT SOCIETY

P.S. Have you been tinkering lately?
We'd love to see your latest invention!

VOTES FOR WOMEN

THE SUFFRAGETTES NEED YOU!

Deeds Not Words!

Join us to get VOTES FOR WOMEN!

Tasks include:

- Delivering the suffragette newspaper
- Attending protests
- Disrupting political speeches
- Causing general mischief*

*Risk of possible prison sentences included

WHY WOMEN SHOULDN'T GET THE VOTE

By Lord George Curzon of Kedleston

(President of the National League for Opposing Woman Suffrage)

See below for some of my valid and incontrovertible arguments against the grant of female suffrage:

1. Will take women away from their duties in the home and to their children
2. Women do not have the correct temperament or intelligence to weigh in on politics
3. Most women do not want to vote
4. Most men do not want women to vote
5. Women probably wouldn't even use the vote
6. If women did vote, they might vote for the wrong person!

TIMELINE

15 July 1858 – Born in Manchester, England

1879 – Marries Richard Pankhurst, a supporter of women's suffrage

1889 – Founds the Women's Franchise League

1903 – Founds the Women's Social and Political Union (WSPU)

1905 – Leads the first WSPU protest in Manchester

1908 – Arrested for protesting

1908–1913 – Arrested at least six more times for suffragette activities

1912 – Goes on multiple hunger strikes in prison to demand better treatment

1913 – The 'Cat and Mouse Act' passes, allowing hunger-strikers to be released from prison, then re-arrested as soon as they recover

8 June 1913 – Fellow protester Emily Davison dies at the London Derby while campaigning for voting rights

1914 – World War One starts – protests are stopped to focus on the war effort. Women encouraged to work in factories

1918 – Representation of the People Act passes, giving some women over 30 the right to vote

14 June 1928 – Dies at age 69

2 July 1928 – The Equal Franchise Act is passed, granting all women over 21 the right to vote in the UK

OFFICIAL MEMO

THE FANTASTICALLY GREAT SOCIETY

FGS HQ
SKY HIGH
HEIGHTS
CH8 NG3

Dear Emmeline,

As one of our earliest members, we're hoping you might find a moment to pass on some of your drive, determination and bravery to our newest recruits. We've always admired not only your incredible leadership, but also how you nurtured others to embrace the many vital roles that kept the suffragette movement running like a well-oiled machine. You showed everyone that there is a place – and a purpose – for all unique skills in the fight for change!

We know you believed in deeds, not words. But just this once, might you share a few lines to remind our recruits that together we are stronger, louder and impossible to ignore? Our members are determined to continue the fight for equality you started. That's why we **VOTE FOR YOU** to give your most rousing speech yet!

Boldly marching with you, sister suffragette,

THE FANTASTICALLY GREAT SOCIETY

P.S. We have been proudly wearing the 'Votes for Women' sashes you sent us!

MANCHESTER
1918
GREAT BRITAIN

Emmeline Pankhurst
Suffragette HQ
United Kingdom

NEPAL
NEPAL
Mt. EVEREST
BRAVE ADVENTURER
BOTTOM OF THE GARDEN
TENT NO. 3
GREAT OUTDOORS
DELIVERED
BY YAK

MEMBER No. 7

EMMELINE PANKHURST

OFFICIAL PORTRAIT
MEMBER NUMBER: 7

The world was a very different place when Emmeline Pankhurst was alive, especially for women. There were lots of things men could do that women weren't allowed to – like vote for who was running the country. Emmeline thought this was very unfair, so she set out to change the law.

Emmeline formed a group of women called 'suffragettes', who campaigned for women's right to vote. The suffragettes' tactics could be quite extreme, including chaining themselves to railings, breaking windows and even setting fires. But Emmeline knew their actions had to be loud in order to be heard. Sometimes they went to prison, but they kept on fighting.

In 1918, the right to vote was given to some women. But Emmeline wanted all women to have that right. So her fight went on. At last, in 1928, shortly after Emmeline's death, the law changed so that all women over 21 could vote. Emmeline's courageous fight paved the way for future generations of women to have a voice in the world.

MEMBERSHIP DETAILS

NOTE: Emmeline liked to incorrectly say that she was born on 14 July as this is 'Bastille Day', a day commemorating the start of the French Revolution. She felt she was born to be a rebel!

NAME: Emmeline Pankhurst

DATE OF BIRTH: ~~14~~ 15 July 1858

NATIONALITY: British

OCCUPATION: Women's rights activist

FAMILY: My politically radical parents, my husband Richard (a fellow supporter!) – and my five children, Christabel, Sylvia, Francis Henry, Adela and Henry Francis

DESCRIBE YOURSELF IN 3 WORDS: Fierce, brave, relentless

GREATEST ACHIEVEMENT: Leading the movement that ensured all women had the right to vote – and having my daughters join, too!

WORLD FIRSTS:
1. Created the first group where women worked together to win the vote through bold, attention-grabbing actions
2. Led the first movement that called its members 'Suffragettes' – a word that became known and used across the world!

FAVOURITE COLOURS: Purple, white and green – these are our suffragette colours and are an important symbol of our fight

FAMOUS WORDS: "Deeds not words!" (This was our motto – sometimes, action is the only way to get people to listen!)

VOTES for WOMEN
GO GIRLS
VOTES
VOTES
VOTES
VOTES
1st
A COURAGEOUS ACTIVIST
Stand Up Lane
THE RAILINGS
EQL R1GTS

OFFICIAL MEMO

THE FANTASTICALLY GREAT SOCIETY

FGS HQ
SKY HIGH
HEIGHTS
CH8 NG3

Dear new recruit,

We trust you have found your recent correspondence with the Fantastically Great Women **enlightening** and **inspiring**! Hold their words close to your heart. They could be useful for overcoming a challenge today, or as you chase your dreams in years to come.

Now, **it's over to you!** We'd like you to start work on a official society **fact file** about **YOUR** fantastical greatness. Enclosed are some questions to use as a starting point. We hope you have fun reflecting on your achievements and brilliance so far. We at the society simply cannot wait to see what you do next!

Brimming with anticipation,

THE FANTASTICALLY GREAT SOCIETY

P.S. You can be fantastically great every day, in every small way. (We know you already are.)

THE FANTASTICALLY GREAT SOCIETY
MEMBERSHIP CARD

MEMBER No.
356, 897, 229

FANTASTIC
RIGHT
NOW
GREATNESS

SOCIETY MEMBER
Your House
Down the Road
INS P1R3